For Emmanuel, whose courage and character are an inspiration —L.A.T.

For Emmanuel and the dreamers —S.Q.

With this publication Random House has made a donation to the charity Emmanuel's Dream.

Text copyright © 2015 by Laurie Ann Thompson
Jacket art and interior illustrations copyright © 2015 by Sean Qualls

All rights reserved. Published in the United States by
Schwartz & Wade Books, an imprint of Random House
Children's Books, a division of Random House LLC,
a Penguin Random House Company, New York.

Schwartz & Wade Books and the colophon are trademarks of
Random House LLC.

Visit us on the Web! randomhousekids.com

Educators and librarians, for a variety of teaching tools, visit us at RHTeachersLibrarians.com

Library of Congress Cataloging-in-Publication Data
Thompson, Laurie Ann.
Emmanuel's dream : the true story of Emmanuel Ofosu Yeboah / by Laurie Ann Thompson ; illustrated by
Sean Qualls.—First edition.   pages cm
ISBN 978-0-449-81744-5 (trade) — ISBN 978-0-449-81745-2 (glb)
ISBN 978-0-449-81746-9 (ebk)
1. Yeboah, Emmanuel Ofosu, 1977– —Juvenile literature. 2. People with disabilities—Ghana—Biography—
Juvenile literature. 3. Cyclists—Ghana—Biography—Juvenile literature. 4. Ghana—Biography—Juvenile
literature. I. Qualls, Sean, illustrator. II. Title.
HV3013.Y43T56 2015
362.4092—dc23
[B]
2014005767

The text of this book is set in Graham.
The illustrations were rendered in mixed media.

MANUFACTURED IN CHINA

10 9 8 7 6 5 4 3 2 1

First Edition

GHANA

EMMANUEL'S DREAM

THE TRUE STORY OF
EMMANUEL OFOSU YEBOAH

KOFORIDUA

ACCRA

BY LAURIE ANN THOMPSON
ILLUSTRATED BY SEAN QUALLS

schwartz & wade books · new york

In Ghana, West Africa, a baby boy was born:

Two bright eyes blinked in the light,

two healthy lungs let out a powerful cry,

two tiny fists opened and closed,

but only one strong leg kicked.

Most people thought he would be useless, or worse—

a curse.

His father left, never to return.

But his mother had faith.

Her name was Comfort,

and she named her first child Emmanuel,

meaning "God is with us."

As Emmanuel grew,

Mama Comfort told him he could have anything,

but he would have to get it for himself.

He learned to crawl and hop,

to fetch water and climb
coconut trees.

He even shined shoes to earn money.

Most kids with disabilities couldn't go to school.
Still, Emmanuel's mother carried him there,
until one day she said, "You are too heavy."

From then on, Emmanuel hopped to school and back,

two miles each way,
on one leg,
by himself.

At first, nobody would play with him.

So Emmanuel saved his money

and bought something none of his classmates had:

a brand-new soccer ball.

Of course he would share it . . .

if he could play, too.

Lunging and spinning on crutches

his grandmother had found for him

and kicking the ball with his good left foot,

Emmanuel earned their respect.

His new friends sometimes used their lunch money to rent bikes.

Would Emmanuel be able to join them?

His friend Godwin pushed him fast so he could balance.

Over and over again, Emmanuel fell—hard—

but finally . . .

he rode!

When Emmanuel was thirteen,

Mama Comfort got very sick.

She could no longer sell vegetables at the market,

and Emmanuel's sister and brother were too little to work.

He would have to support them.

Against his mother's wishes, Emmanuel snuck out
and boarded a midnight train to the bustling city of Accra,
one hundred and fifty miles away,
alone.

He didn't know it then, but it would be two years
before he saw his family again.

Emmanuel arrived full of hope:
There were so many people!
But no one would hire him.

Shopkeepers and restaurant owners
told him to go out and beg
like other disabled people did.
Emmanuel refused.
Finally, a food stand owner offered him a job—
and a place to live.

When Emmanuel wasn't serving drinks,
he kept busy shining shoes.
He earned money
and sent it home.

One morning when Emmanuel went to buy shoe-shining supplies,
the shopkeeper thought he was there to beg
and scolded him.
Insulted, Emmanuel slammed his money
down on the counter.
The shopkeeper apologized,
but Emmanuel would never forget.

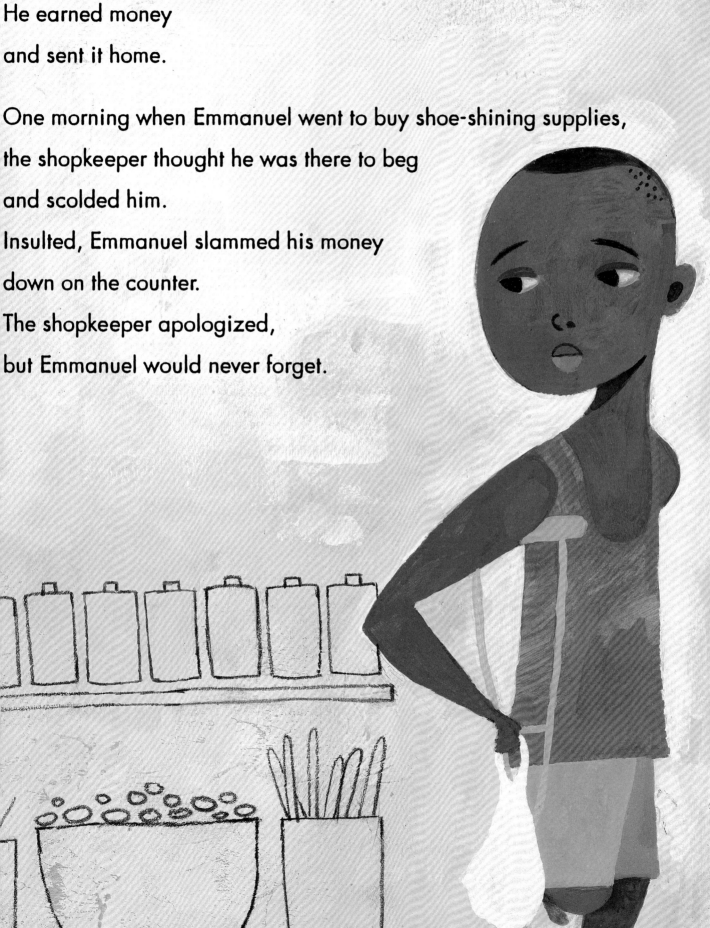

When Mama Comfort grew sicker,

Emmanuel went home to be with her.

From her bed on Christmas Eve she told her son,

"Be respectful, take care of your family, don't ever beg.

And don't give up."

By the next morning,

Emmanuel's beloved mother was dead.

He was heartbroken, but he knew

her last words had been a gift.

He would honor them by showing everyone

that being disabled does not mean

being *un*able.

It was a big dream,

but Emmanuel had a plan.

Emmanuel had a sharp mind,
a bold heart,
and one strong leg.

All he needed was a bike.

At first no one would help.
They thought his plan,
to bicycle around Ghana,
was impossible.

Then Emmanuel wrote to the Challenged Athletes Foundation,
all the way in San Diego, California.

They sent him a bike . . . plus a helmet, shorts, socks, and gloves!

Emmanuel started training for the long ride.

He persuaded the king of his region to give him a royal blessing.

He went door to door asking for additional support.

Finally, he hired a taxi to follow him with drinking water, a camera,

and his best friends.

Then Emmanuel tied his right leg to the bike's frame,

jammed his left foot into a flip-flop attached to the pedal,

and rode.

Emmanuel pedaled through the bustling city of Accra.

He pedaled through rain forests,

over rolling hills,

and across wide, muddy rivers.

He pedaled past odum forests and plantain farms

and through the market city of Kumasi.

He pedaled as trucks roared past on the narrow highways

and wild animals stalked his thoughts.

He pedaled through vast grasslands

and into the ancient city of Tamale.

He rode up, down, across, and around his country,

proudly wearing the colors of its flag

on a shirt printed with the words THE POZO,

or "the disabled person."

Along the way, Emmanuel talked
to those with physical challenges and those without,
to poor farm workers and wealthy landowners,
to religious leaders, government officials, and reporters.

THE POZO

He wanted everyone to see him—
and his disability.
He wanted everyone to hear him—
and his message.

The farther Emmanuel rode,

the more attention he got.

Children cheered.

Able-bodied adults ran or rode along with him.

People with disabilities left their homes and came outside,

some for the very first time.

The young man once thought of as cursed

was becoming a national hero.

He completed his astounding journey,
pedaling south to the sea and back up to Accra—
nearly four hundred miles—in just ten days.

But Emmanuel's success goes even further than that.
He proved that one leg is enough to do great things—
and one person is enough to change the world.

"In this world, we are not perfect. We can only do our best."

—Emmanuel Ofosu Yeboah

Author's Note

Emmanuel still isn't giving up. Since completing his first long-distance bike ride across Ghana in 2001 at the age of twenty-four, he has competed in major athletic events, won international awards from Nike and ESPN, and carried the Olympic torch in Cairo, Egypt, in 2004. He starred in a documentary about his life called *Emmanuel's Gift*, and he appeared on *The Oprah Winfrey Show*.

In 2006, thanks in large part to Emmanuel's bike ride and his continued political activism, the Ghanaian Parliament passed the Persons with Disability Act, which states that people with physical disabilities are entitled to all of the same rights as the rest of the country's citizens. "I am very happy for my disabled brothers and sisters in Ghana," said Emmanuel, "[but] this is just the beginning."

Today, Emmanuel continues to work on behalf of the disabled. He maintains a scholarship fund to help children with disabilities attend school, and he helps organizations distribute wheelchairs to those in need. In addition, he works closely with Ghana's government to pass laws protecting the rights of disabled citizens, and he speaks to political leaders, independent organizations, and schoolchildren around the world to deliver the message that disability does *not* mean inability.

To find out more about Emmanuel and his activities, including the progress of the school he is building for children with and without disabilities, please visit the Emmanuel Educational Foundation and Sports Academy (EEFSA) website at EmmanuelsDream.org.

Idaho

BY MARI KESSELRING

The Child's World

Published by The Child's World®
1980 Lookout Drive • Mankato, MN 56003-1705
800-599-READ • www.childsworld.com

ACKNOWLEDGMENTS
The Child's World®: Mary Berendes, Publishing Director
The Design Lab: Design and production
Red Line Editorial: Editorial direction

PHOTO CREDITS: Wojtek Kryczka/iStockphoto, cover, 1, 3; Matt Kania/Map Hero, Inc., 4, 5; Christian Nafzger/iStockphoto, 7; Shutterstock Images, 9, iStockphoto, 10; Marjorie McBride/ Idaho Stock Images, 11; Denton Rumsey/ Shutterstock Images, 13, North Wind Pictures/Photolibrary, 15; Emily Ryan/ iStockphoto, 17; Peter Dejong/AP Images, 19; Shutterstock Images, 21; One Mile Up, 22; Quarter-dollar coin image from the United States Mint, 22

LIBRARY OF CONGRESS CATALOGING-IN-PUBLICATION DATA
Kesselring, Mari.
  Idaho / by Mari Kesselring.
      p. cm.
  Includes bibliographical references and index.
  ISBN 978-1-60253-456-8 (library bound : alk. paper)
  1. Idaho—Juvenile literature. I. Title.

F746.3.K47 2010
979.6—dc22

                                        2010017675

Printed in the United States of America in Mankato, Minnesota.
July 2010
F11538

On the cover:
Many farmers
in Idaho grow
potatoes.

CONTENTS

Geography

Let's explore Idaho! Idaho is in the northwest United States. It shares its short, northern border with Canada.

WASHINGTON

MONTANA

NORTH
WEST • EAST
SOUTH

Wallace

Rocky Mountains

Lewiston

Hells
Canyon

Snake River

Salmon

McCall

IDAHO

Yellowstone
National Park

Borah Peak

OREGON

Boise River

★ **Boise**

Sun Valley

Arco

Idaho
Falls

Blackfoot

Pocatello

WYOMING

Shoshone
Falls

Twin Falls

NEVADA

UTAH

Cities

Boise is the capital of Idaho. It is also the largest city. It is next to the Boise River. Sun Valley, Idaho Falls, and Pocatello are other large cities in the state.

Boise is in southwestern Idaho. ▶

Land

The Rocky Mountains run through about half of Idaho. The highest mountain in Idaho is Borah Peak. **Plateaus**, **prairies**, and valleys are found in this state. Idaho also has about 2,000 lakes. The Snake River runs through the southern part of the state.

Wildflowers grow in the valleys near the Rocky Mountains. ▶

Plants and Animals

Forests cover less than half of Idaho. The state tree is the western white pine. It stays green all year. Grizzly bears and gray wolves live in some **wilderness** areas of Idaho. The state bird is the mountain bluebird. The state flower is the syringa. It has small white **petals**.

The syringa became the Idaho state flower in 1931. ▶

People and Work

About 1.5 million people live in Idaho. The land is often used to raise cattle or to farm. Many people work in **logging**. They cut down trees for wood. People also work in **tourism**.

More potatoes are grown in Idaho than in any other state.

Potatoes are grown on this farm in Idaho. ▶

History

Native Americans were the first people to live in the Idaho area. The Shoshone was one of the biggest **tribes**. Many settlers arrived by wagons in the 1840s. Idaho became the forty-third state on July 3, 1890.

The name "Idaho" is from the Shoshone language. It means "gem of the mountains."

Some settlers traveling to Idaho had to cross the Snake River. ▶

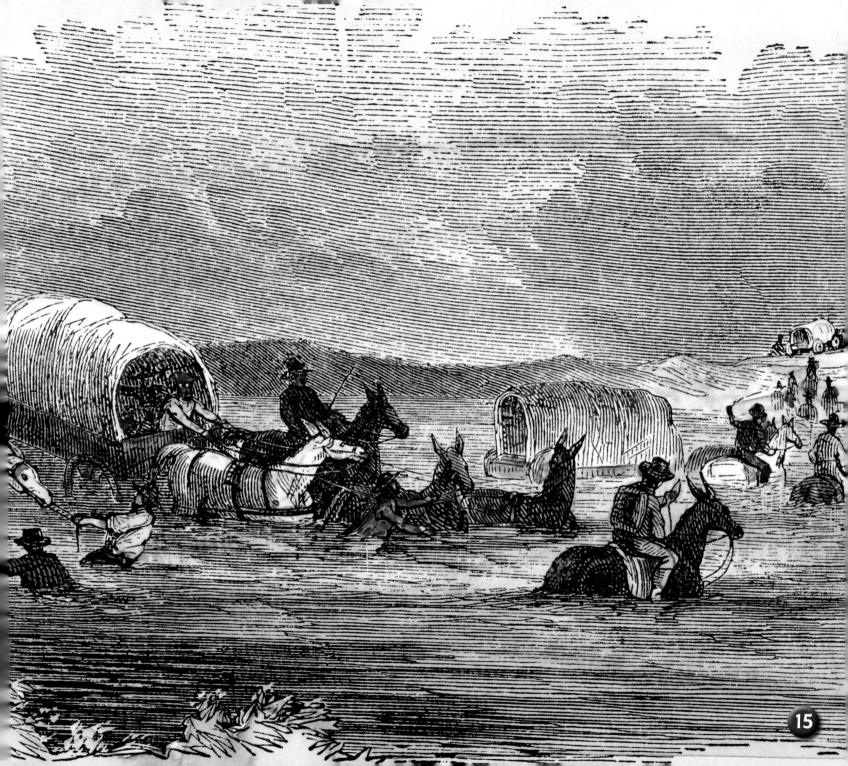

Ways of Life

Religion is important to many people who live in Idaho. About a third of the people practice the Mormon religion. The religion is also called the Church of Jesus Christ of Latter-day Saints. Many people enjoy hunting and fishing. Idaho's mountains also make it a great place for skiing.

Boating and water skiing are **popular** in Idaho. ▶

Famous People

Olympic skier Picabo (PEEK-a-boo) Street was born in a small Idaho town. Sacagawea was born here, too. She was a Shoshone Indian who helped Meriwether Lewis and William Clark explore the West.

Picabo Street skied in three Olympic Winter Games. ▶ She won one gold medal and one silver medal.

Picabo Street was named after the small town of Picabo, Idaho.

Famous Places

Idaho has many parks and campgrounds. Part of Yellowstone National Park is in Idaho. Sun Valley, Idaho, is a popular place for ski trips. Shoshone Falls is a popular waterfall to see.

Shoshone Falls is 212 feet (64.6 m) tall. ▶

State Symbols

Seal

The people on the Idaho state seal stand for liberty and mining. The fruits and vegetables at the bottom of the seal stand for farming. Go to childsworld.com/links for a link to Idaho's state Web site, where you can get a firsthand look at the state seal.

Flag

The seal is on the state flag. The elk's head at the top of the seal shows the importance of hunting.

Quarter

The Idaho state quarter shows the peregrine falcon, a common Idaho bird. The phrase "Esto Perpetua" is the state's **motto**. It means "May it be Forever" in the Latin language. The quarter came out in 2007.

Glossary

gem (JEM): A gem is a precious stone. Idaho means "gem of the mountains."

logging (LOG-ing): Logging is cutting down trees to use for lumber or other wood products. People in Idaho work in logging.

motto (MOT-oh): A motto is a sentence that states what people stand for or believe. Idaho's motto means "May it be Forever."

petals (PET-ulz): Petals are the colorful parts of flowers. Idaho's state flower has white petals.

plateaus (pla-TOHZ): Plateaus are flat areas on the tops of hills or mountains. Idaho has some plateaus.

popular (POP-yuh-lur): To be popular is to be enjoyed by many people. Outdoor activities are popular in Idaho.

prairies (PRAYR-eez): Prairies are flat or hilly grasslands. There are some prairies in Idaho.

religion (reh-LIJ-un): Religion is a system of beliefs about God or gods. Many people in Idaho practice the Mormon religion.

seal (SEEL): A seal is a symbol a state uses for government business. One part of Idaho's seal shows the importance of farming.

symbols (SIM-bulz): Symbols are pictures or things that stand for something else. The seal and flag are Idaho's symbols.

tourism (TOOR-ih-zum): Tourism is visiting another place (such as a state or country) for fun or the jobs that help these visitors. Some people in Idaho work in tourism.

tribes (TRYBZ): Tribes are groups of people who share ancestors and customs. The Shoshone was one of the Native American tribes in Idaho.

wilderness (WILL-der-ness): Wilderness is an area of land where no people live. Idaho has many wilderness areas.

Further Information

Books

Kent, Deborah. *Idaho*. New York: Children's Press, 2009.

Steiner, Joy, and Stan Steiner. *P is for Potato: An Idaho Alphabet*. Chelsea, MI: Sleeping Bear Press, 2005.

Zollman, Pam. *Idaho*. New York: Children's Press, 2006.

Web Sites

Visit our Web site for links about Idaho: *childsworld.com/links*

Note to Parents, Teachers, and Librarians: We routinely verify our Web links to make sure they are safe and active sites. So encourage your readers to check them out!

Index